VODOU

Vodou

Manuela Dunn Mascetti

CHRONICLE BOOKS

SAN FRANCISCO

6/12

TEXT BY *Manuela Dunn Mascetti*
DESIGN BY *Bullet Liongson*
MANUFACTURED IN *China*
TYPESET IN *Celestiu Antiqua*

ISBN 0-8118-3109-4

Distributed in Canada by
RAINCOAST BOOKS
9050 Shaughnessy Street
Vancouver, B.C. V6P 6E5

10 9 8 7 6 5 4 3 2 1

CHRONICLE BOOKS LLC
85 Second Street
San Francisco, CA 94105
www.chroniclebooks.com

BL
2490
M37
2002

Table of Contents

7 INTRODUCTION

13 THE GREAT CROSSING
 The Ancient Kingdom of Dahomey
 Saint Domingue

31 THE DANCED RELIGION

45 THE SPIRITS OF VODOU
 Papa Legba
 Ogou the Red
 Bhatalah
 Baron Samdi and the Gédé Family
 Agwé and the Simbi
 Damballah-wèdo and Aida-wèdo
 Ezili
 The Twins

65 THE VODOU ALTAR

71 THE VODOU RITUAL
 The Vodou Service

81 MAKE YOUR OWN VODOU ALTAR
 Building Your Altar
 Preparing for the Rituals
 Spirit Bottle Ritual

93 FURTHER READING

94 ART ACKNOWLEDGMENTS

Introduction

VODOU has only recently shaken off the negative connotations
that tainted it hundreds of years ago. For many years associated
with dolls, pins, and black magic, it is today being revalued as the
true religion it is. Vodou was born from the animist religions of
West Africa and includes a vast pantheon of deities and spirits
who constantly involve themselves in the affairs of humans. The
word *animism* means "ensouled," and animist religions honor the
presence of soul everywhere: in trees, rivers, stones, forests, fields,
and mountains. Vodou also honors the presence of the soul
within the human body—when one falls ill, it is believed to be
because a spirit has entered one's diseased body—and teaches
that spirits are everywhere, commingling with our lives.

The people of Togo, Benin, Niger, Nigeria, and the Ivory
Coast still practice Vodou today in its original form. From birth
to death, they are accompanied by spirits who tell them everything: what their destiny is, why things happen the way they
do, why they have fallen ill, who they will marry, and when—
and often why—they are going to die.

A strongly prejudiced notion of Vodou classes the religion as
a dangerous practice of sorcery in which animal and sometimes

7

human sacrifice is used. Such sorcery was rumored to awaken the dead from their graves and transform them into zombies. This morbid and hallucinatory depiction of Vodou is especially found in late nineteenth-century books on Haiti by American and European authors, who described blood-curdling crimes committed by deranged Vodou priests in the frenzy of trance and possession by evil spirits. Many of these writers depicted Vodou as a cannibalistic religion, and Haiti as a savage country where thousands of children were sacrificed every year and devoured by the monstrous worshipers of the Serpent.

These strange and frightening tales, however, belong to the past. They have more to do with the fear and lack of understanding that slaveholders felt toward their slaves. To assuage their guilt over the crimes they perpetrated for centuries on the people of West Africa, many slaveholders demonized the slaves, deeming their religion something to be suppressed and exterminated. These old attitudes have nothing to do with the true spirit of the Vodou religion—nor with any knowledge of its actual practices.

Today Vodou—and its adaptions and expansions—is finally emerging from prejudice and persecution, and is being recognized as one of the most powerful cultural movements not only in Haiti, the capital of Vodou, but also in the United States, Brazil, Cuba, and the Caribbean.

In Haiti it has inspired a unique, world-renowned form of painting, which the critic André Malraux described in 1975 as "the most thrilling experience—and the only one that can be verified—of magical painting in our century." Haitian painting draws its power from the Vodou pantheon. In Vodou liturgy, each color is associated with a *loa*, or deity, and in painting, the colors become the meeting place of spirit and matter. Vertical lines represent the spirit, and horizontal lines the world of humans. The circle is not only the symbol for Damballah, one of the main deities, but also of the Vodou notion that we are the center of everything.

Stylized Vodou dances have also gained popularity and are often referred to simply as "African dance." However, many of the gestures and movements trace their origin to the sacred expressions of spirit possession. Music is another stirring expression of the religion that is gaining recognition through roots-groups who demonstrate the positive cultural values of Vodou. We are learning to see the influence of Vodou on classic literature such as *Huckleberry Finn*, on African-American art, and on the creativity of entire chapters of twentieth-century music: tango, samba, rumba, jazz, blues, and soul.

Vodou is, above all, about honoring the spirit that inhabits every living form in our world. Vodou rituals and objects are crafted to honor that spirit and to promote well-being, healing, good fortune, good prospects, and everything that adds positive change to one's life.

The spirit bottle you find in this box is among the most popular and enduring symbols of Vodou. Spirit bottles have been used for centuries by Vodou practitioners for spiritual embottlement: calling the spirits into a sacred space in order to ask questions and to receive answers.

Place the spirit bottle on the nightstand by your bed, on your home altar, on your desk at work, or wherever it looks beautiful. Every time you look at it, allow it to remind you that spirits are vitally present in our everyday lives; they are close to us and can relieve some of our concerns and fears. Ideally, the spirit bottle should sit peacefully in an empty space. Its bright and beautiful colors will attract Vodou spirits who will empower it, and their essence will be kept safely within it.

Vodou enfolds all things and all beings. The spirit bottle is a reminder of the strong, positive, and rich power of the *loa*.

May the spirit of Vodou be with you and guide you through challenging life decisions and past obstacles to a life of happiness.

The Great Crossing

CONTRARY TO COMMON BELIEF, Vodou is not a malicious, perfidious practice of harming others by sticking pins in magic dolls. It has a rich and ancient cosmology that manifests itself through rituals, songs, language, dances, and symbolic objects. Vodou is a vibrant cultural force that traces its deep roots to the countries of West Africa, where it first developed many centuries ago. Its history goes hand in hand with the history of arguably the most brutal treatment of humans by other humans—the slave trade. As such the history of this religion includes ghastly and disquieting chapters, the grim echoes of which are intertwined with the soul of a people who were stripped of dignity and yet found a new sense of identity and hope in the practice of Vodou.

When the tribes of the Gulf of Guinea were captured and sold into slavery by their own neighbors—the kings of Dahomey (today the Republic of Benin)—the Vodou gods traveled with them to the New World. From the plantations in Haiti, Vodou spread everywhere the people of West Africa were taken. The *loa* have thrived in Brazil for centuries under the name of Candomblé. The hometown of Candomblé is Bahia, one of the original ports of the slave trade. This form of Vodou has spread inland, and today

it is practiced as far away as São Paulo. Candomblé preserves all the Yoruba (a West African language) names of the gods and words in its incantations, and honors Oxalà as its principal deity. Vodou is also practiced in the Haitian diaspora, which includes the Dominican Republic, the United States, Canada, the French-speaking Caribbean, and France. The *loa* travel with priests and priestesses and have become established in Vodou churches and congregations around the world. In Brooklyn, for instance, there are several Vodou practitioners who heal everything from bad luck to the misfortunes of an accident, a lost job, a robbery, financial troubles, or an illness. In New Orleans, Vodou priestesses make sacred ritual objects that are sold around the world. Vodou today is a source of fascination, having finally emerged from centuries of obscurity.

THE ANCIENT KINGDOM OF DAHOMEY

In the nineteenth century the Kingdom of Dahomey was a Black Sparta squeezed between the Yoruba tribes of present-day Nigeria and the Ewe tribes of Togo. Her kings had claw marks cut on their temples and were descended from a princess of Adja-Tado and the leopard who seduced her on the banks of the Mono River. Their people called them "Dada," which means "father" in Fon. Their fiercest regiments were female, and their only source of income was the sale of their weaker neighbors.

—Bruce Chatwin, *The Viceroy of Ouidah*

The Sub-Saharan countries that are the ancestral home of Vodou are the regions of West Africa that include Dahomey, Togo, Nigeria, Niger, Mali, Angola, and Liberia. The nature-based religions of West Africa have a strongly spiritualized ecology whose spirits have never been driven into oblivion by the advent of urbanization. Spirits are believed to reside everywhere in the natural world—in trees, groves, and mounds; in pools of water, inside caves, at natural crossroads. They manifest in the world of humans and meddle in their affairs, presiding over all activities and overseeing all realms of nature. In Fon, the native language of Benin, *Vodou* means god, spirit, and sacred object—the place where a spirit or a god manifests or resides. Europeans erroneously translated the word *vodou* as "fetish," whereas for the Fon, Ewe, and Yoruba tribes of West Africa, it means sacredness. Fon society is organized around the ethnic group, the village, the family, and kinship. Each of these groups has its own *vodu*, ancestral guardian deities who protect the people, animals, and nature.

Far from primitive, the animist religions of West Africa were rich and full of subtleties. The supernatural world gravitated around a main deity—Mawu—and other gods related to him grouped in pantheons and hierarchies. There were also other ancillary divine beings: ancestors of clans, gods of vassal tribes, and monsters. Music and dance were so closely interwoven into the cults and practices that Vodou has been called the "danced

religion." Both music and dance are believed to be gifts of the gods. Trancelike states are where the boundary between the human and the divine disappears, and where spirits can possess an individual to bring messages and healing. Gods are also represented by sacred symbols or fetishes: stones, branches, plants, vases, bits and pieces found in nature, handmade figurines, straw, bones, leather, rags, fur, feathers, and blood. Centuries ago, white people regarded these sacred objects as a "garbage heap"; ironically, today West African art has become highly collectible throughout the world. However, these objects were not designed to display purity and abstract beauty, but rather as the means of transference of human desire, conflict, illness, suffering, life, birth, and death. The priests who empower these objects with divine essence in order to cure or reestablish harmony are believed to be direct descendants of the gods themselves, an ancestral lineage that has been in service since the beginning of time and that cannot be broken.

Tension had always existed among the various clans and tribal groups of West Africa, marked by conflicts and wars. The kings of Dahomey, seeking to expand their power, carried out a series of raids into neighboring tribes, centralizing the powers of Vodou into their own hands by subjugating their enemies' deities, controlling their priests, and enslaving prisoners of war. In 1492, the Spanish conquered the island of Haiti in the archipelago of the Antilles. The local Taino and Arawak tribes called

the island Haiti to describe its mountainous geography, the Spanish renamed it Hispaniola. The local population, which had been estimated at 1.3 million at the beginning of the sixteenth century, was decimated within decades by cruel treatment, illness, and forced labor in the gold mines.

The Spanish needed fresh supplies of laborers to work on the island. In 1517, Charles V authorized the importation of fifteen thousand black slaves. A small contingent of French travelers also settled on the Spanish island of Tortuga, just north of Hispaniola. Little by little, through fighting the Spanish, the French gained a foothold on a corner of Hispaniola. This land was eventually ceded to France by Spain in 1697 with the Treaty of Ryswick, and the French renamed it Saint Domingue. Sugar plantations were the main industry of both Saint Domingue and Hispaniola, and the high demand for laborers brought about the beginning of the slave trade and Europe's Golden Age.

The slavers carried out their business in the Gulf of Guinea, called the Slave Coast, well into the early-twentieth century. The traders conducted transactions mainly with the royal family of Dahomey, whose capital was Ouidah (spelled *Whydah* by the British and *Ajuda*, meaning "help," by the Portuguese). The Dahomey royals were eager for European products—arms, glass beads, cotton materials, metal, and brandy. Between 1710 and 1810 more than a million slaves were captured in the Gulf

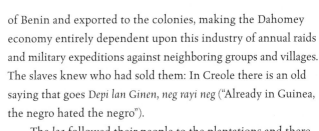

of Benin and exported to the colonies, making the Dahomey economy entirely dependent upon this industry of annual raids and military expeditions against neighboring groups and villages. The slaves knew who had sold them: In Creole there is an old saying that goes *Depi lan Ginen, neg rayi neg* ("Already in Guinea, the negro hated the negro").

The *loa* followed their people to the plantations and there rooted themselves in the soil and life of the New World, forming a new pantheon.

SAINT DOMINGUE

The king went to war in January and the chain gangs started reaching Ouidah toward the end of March.

The captives were numb with fright and exhaustion. They had seen their homes burned and their chiefs slaughtered. Iron collars chafed their necks. Their backs were striped purple with welts; and when they saw the white man's ships, they knew they were going to be eaten.

—Bruce Chatwin, The Viceroy of Ouidah

The slave trade had dire consequences, not just for those who were captured and taken into slavery but also for those who escaped the raids. Those fortunate enough to flee from enslavement returned home to find their farms burned, their granaries emptied, their animals stolen or slaughtered, their temples destroyed. The prime targets of the slave raids were young men and women, who would have been essential in providing the labor to rebuild and sustain the community, and without whom the survival of the clans was tenuous. Their situation would have been intolerable had they not held supreme faith in the gods of Vodou. Vodou helped them cope with the difficult conditions and great misfortunes that faced the tribes of West Africa, and helped their captured kin cope with their new lives on the plantations.

Because the Kingdom of Dahomey was so dependent upon the slave trade, the royal family reached deeper and deeper into neighboring countries in order to supply British, Spanish, Portuguese, and French slavers. As a consequence, many different tribes arrived in Saint Domingue. The majority were Fon from Dahomey and Yoruba from Nigeria, but there were also Senegalese, Congolese, Minas, and people from many other ethnic groups. Each of these groups had their own gods, spirits, and practices, but Vodou was the one cultural thread they had in common in spite of linguistic differences and tribal antagonism.

The plantations on Saint Domingue, Hispaniola, and the other islands of the Spanish Caribbean were producing proletarian and urban commodities that were in high demand in Europe: sugar, tobacco, coffee, and rum. There was plenty of capital to finance the slave trade, bringing new humans as property to the

flourishing plantations. It is estimated that Saint Domingue alone received about 900,000 slaves in its history as a plantation colony. West Africans came across the waters in primitive eighteenth-century sea craft, enduring horrific passages. Many died en route. Those who did survive the journey were divided from their kin; sold off at auctions to different plantation owners (systematically mixing ethnic groups); given new names by their owners; and subjugated to such intense physical labor that their lives were estimated to last not more than ten years after enslavement. This system was meant to make the slaves lose all memory of family, lineage, origins, and religion.

To the white plantation owners, Vodou was a form of witch-craft whose evil idols, devils, fetishes, and black magic were highly dangerous. The original Vodou fetishes and statuettes they saw must have been very similar to the sacred artifacts one finds in West Africa today. Made of wood and decorated with natural materials such as leather, leaves, shells, and vegetable dyes, these sacred statues look "primitive" and rural—fitting for peaceful agrarian tribes. In comparison to the glorious paintings of Christianity, Vodou statuettes must have looked strange, foreign, and malevolent. Just as those who practiced ancient nature-based religions in Europe were persecuted in "witch hunts," Vodou practitioners were demonized and punished from the very beginning of plantation history. The belief that Vodou practices were a form of black magic intended to harm whites helped absolve many slave owners of the heinousness of their crimes.

The Roman Catholic Church justified the slave trade by arguing that it was converting and saving the slaves. Adding new converts to the faith was seen as morally right, as it furthered God's mission on earth. Louis XIII had stipulated that any slave the Compagnie Française des Isles d'Amerique (founded in 1635 to carry on the trade) took to France's colonies had to be baptized and instructed in the Catholic religion. The Code Noir, or "Black Code," the official guidelines for slavery, gave precise justification to the position of the Church in terms of the slave trade. Article 2 stipulates, "All the slaves in our islands will be baptized and instructed in the Catholic religion, apostolic and Roman." Article 3 insists, "The public practice of all religion except Catholicism is forbidden . . . ."

To prevent the practice of African religious traditions, the code also outlawed any gathering of slaves, night or day. It regulated the slaves' every activity—work, rest, family—and classed them as personal property, leaving them no rights.

The Danced Religion

Lying awake one night, he heard a sound of drumbeats in the hills. He
dressed and followed the sound to a forest clearing where some slaves
were calling their gods across the Atlantic. The dancers wore white
metal masks and white dresses that glowed orange in the firelight.
They whirled round and round until Exu the Messenger tapped them
between their shoulder blades. Then, one by one, they shuddered,
growled, crumpled at the knees and fell to the ground in silence.
—Bruce Chatwin, *The Viceroy of Ouidah*

THE SPIRIT of the African animist religions was not easily subjugated, despite the rulings of the Code Noir and the compulsory
baptism of slaves. Torn from their roots and treated brutally by
their masters, the African men and women in the colonies
resumed their cultural and religious practices in extreme secrecy.
Worship of their gods represented individual and collective
strength, and helped them reestablish a form of integrity in the
new environment. In order to hide their now-forbidden religious
practices, the African priests and priestesses used elements of
Catholicism as a screen for animist gods and rituals. A completely
new version of the original religion emerged. Catholic saints,

sacraments, the liturgy, the holy calendar—even baptism, holy processions, and altars—became a part of Vodou. Father Labat, an early observer and chronicler of life in the plantations, stated in his book *Nouveau Voyage aux Iles de l'Amerique* ("New Voyage to the Islands of America"), "The Negros do without a qualm what the Philistines did: they put Dagon with the Ark and secretly preserve all the superstitions of their ancient idolatrous cult alongside the ceremonies of Christianity." This would provoke the wrath and indignation of the Church against Haiti when it was finally discovered how Christianity had been masquerading Vodou for hundreds of years.

The Code Noir forbade the gathering of slaves for religious purposes because the whites considered animism a form of sorcery. Slaves who were found in possession of Vodou objects and amulets were punished with lashings, imprisonment, hangings, and blanchings (the laying bare, with a knife, of the white tissues under the skin). Slavery almost completely destroyed the craftsmanship and artistic skills the African people had arrived with. Art, sculpture, crafts, and painting were then, as they still are today, among the main expressions of African life, but in the colonies no art was produced for fear that the white masters would consider it Vodou or fetishist—and would punish the artist and destroy the object.

Slaves began to gather under the ruse that they were practicing Catholicism. At night, in forest clearings surrounding the

plantations, they renewed their rites with drumming, chanting, and dancing. The dancing was perhaps the most disturbing element to the few white people who witnessed these events, because it was practiced as a form of "divine possession" through which a divinity would enter the body of the priest or priestess and communicate with the faithful, who stood in a wide circle. The sacrificial blood flowing from slain animals would be poured onto the participants. These trances would then extend to the faithful and, to the furious beat of the drums, everyone would spin around and fall into a state of possession.

In a 1760 manuscript entitled *Essay on Slavery*, the phenomenon of the dance-trance is described in detail: "The dance known in Surinam as *Water Maman*, and in our colonies as *La mère de l'eau*, is strictly forbidden. They build into a great mystery, and the only thing known about it is that it greatly heats their imagination. They work themselves up to a frenzy whenever they contemplate some mischief. The ringleader goes into a trance of ecstasy. When he comes to himself, he says his god has spoken to him and told him what to do; but since none of them have the same god they fall out and spy on each other, and this kind of project is nearly always betrayed."

Many of these eighteenth-century writings on early Vodou are tinged with prejudice and scorn. However, when these quoted passages are read without the bias of an eighteenth-century

mindset, they reveal some Vodou practices that were imported to the New World directly from West Africa, and others that have remained practically unchanged from plantation days until today and are still part of contemporary Vodou religious ceremonies in the African Americas. Perhaps the most accurate and well-known descriptions of eighteenth-century Vodou rituals are found in Moreau de Saint-Méry's book *Description of the French Part of Saint Domingue*, where the word *vaudou* is translated as "an all-powerful and supernatural being," and identified as "the snake under whose auspices gather all who share the faith." In his book, Saint-Méry goes on to say that the snake (*vaudou*) will not give of its power or make known its will except through a high priest or priestess known as "king or queen, master or mistress, or even *papa* or *maman*." The Vodou priests are called *hungan* or *mambo* and are the recognized leaders of the "vodou family," as the congregation is known, whose members must pay the priests unlimited respect. The priest or priestess decides whether the snake approves the admission of a candidate to the society, which sets out the duties and tasks he or she must fulfill. The priest or priestess also receives the gifts and libations that the snake-divinity expects as its due. To disobey or resist the priest or priestess is equated with disobeying the snake itself and courting dire misfortune.

Snake worship had been practiced for decades in Ouidah, the capital of today's Republic of Benin, where a snake palace can still be visited. When I visited the Snake Palace in 1986, it housed thousands of snakes and its guardian was an old priestess. Today, Vodou worships Damballah-wédo, the serpent-god, who is no longer represented by a living snake but by highly stylized drawings. The report from Saint-Méry shows that Vodou was quite African in character to begin with, but, once it took root in the plantations, it slowly transformed itself into something quite new. For the slaves, Vodou amounted to an escape from the difficulties of their lives and a form of resistance—by magical means—to the oppression enforced by their owners. When the plantation masters eventually figured out that the night gatherings had nothing to do with Catholicism, but were instead Vodou rituals, the law of Haiti was changed to disallow "all gathering of Negros." The ceremonies not only persisted in even greater secrecy, but Vodou took root and grew into a force that would eventually have political dimensions in the slaves' struggle for freedom in Haiti.

Vodou became the new syncretic religion of the slave plantations. All the different tribes and clans from West Africa combined their respective traditions into one that kept the beliefs and rituals of the home continent alive. As the slave trade extended from Hispaniola and Haiti throughout the Antilles, the Caribbean,

and the Americas, so too did Vodou. Today, the equivalents of Vodou in Brazil and Cuba are respectively called Candomblé and Santería. Both are essentially the same in character as Vodou, but have developed different pantheons of gods and distinct forms of worship, songs, rituals, and altars.

Vodou has been most extensively chronicled in Haiti, where it has been written about from the very beginning of the slave trade until today. It is Haitian Vodou that will be the focus of this book. It is also the traditional Haitian spelling of *Vodou* (rather than *Vodoun* or the more contemporary *Voodoo*) that we have chosen to use.

In Haiti, Vodou gathered strength when it became the common bond of runaway slaves, known as Maroons, who started to flee the plantations in ever-increasing numbers as early as the sixteenth century. Vodou fostered a sense of common identity in slaves from different backgrounds and from different plantations: dances, songs, mythology, rituals, and medicinal treatments helped to form kinship structures and new bonds among those whose main goal was to rise in revolt and to abolish slavery.

From 1750 until 1791, many slave masters in Haiti lived in terror of the upsurges of the Maroon leaders, who, led by their powerful "magical sorcery," prophesied the extermination of white supremacy and the liberation of the slaves. One of the best-known black revolt leaders was François Makandal, who

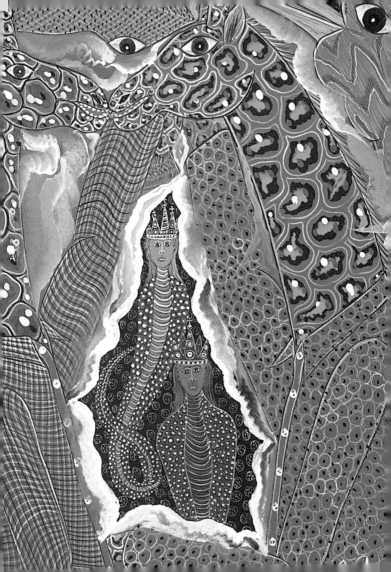

spread fear by poisoning white officials all over the colony and by arming slaves with Vodou talismans that allegedly would make them invulnerable to weapons and that would free them from all fear of white people. Today, the Creole word *makandal* means poison or talisman. The French Revolution led to the abolition of slavery in 1794, and Haiti gained independence from France in 1804, but not before massive rebellions destroyed most of the plantations.

Vodou is the one cultural force that survived the passage from freedom to bondage to freedom for the West African slaves and their descendents. One could say that a curious result of the slave trade was the exaltation and proliferation of the ancient African animist religion: as the slaves were spread, so too was their religion. Today it is practiced in many countries geographically distant from Africa—from Saint Domingue to New York, from Martinique to Brazil—allowing the West African diaspora to maintain a close spiritual bond to their homeland.

The Spirits of Vodou

VODOU IS CHARACTERIZED by an almost infinite variety of gods, goddesses, and spirits, as well as elements of Catholicism, that are part of every ceremony and characterize many rituals. Some of these are old gods of Africa, others developed in the colonies, and still others have arisen since colonial times. Some are almost nondescript, local demons and spirits who vary according to the different regions where Vodou is practiced.

The gods and goddesses are called *loa* or *lwa*, and are more akin to the demons of classical Greek mythology than to actual gods with almighty powers. They are beings who can enter the human body and are found in all realms of nature: in trees, streams, and mountains; in the air, water, wood, and fire. They mediate between the world of the living and the world of the ancestral spirits, between the visible and the invisible. The *loa* also supervise agriculture, war, courtships, births, deaths, and many aspects of the natural world. Natural calamities such as floods and tornadoes are believed to be caused by infuriated *loa*. The *loa* create the structure of time and space, and control the lives of everyone from birth to death. It is thus crucial for priests and priestesses to be able to interpret the wish of the *loa* and

for the faithful to continually pay homage and honor these important spirits.

Lesser but equally ubiquitous spirits are called *mystères*. They generally have such names as Ti-pété, Ti-wawé, and Cinq-jours-malheureux (Unhappy-for-Five-Days). The *loa* can be considered the aristocrats of the Vodou gods, while the *mystères* are the helpers and minor spirits. The Vodou pantheon is always enriching itself with new *mystères* who appear by entering someone's body, stating their name, and demanding to be worshiped. They can also appear in dreams, or travel with a priest or priestess from one location to another.

The *loa* came from a mystical place, believed to be in Guinea, that is considered the fatherland of the Vodou gods. A revelation descended from this mystical region into the spirits and hearts of the African animists who established the religion. The revelation was passed on through two serpents—Dambhalah-wèdo and Aida-wèdo—who represent an almighty ancestor, a supreme personage who was the first of the living. This mystical home is also the ancestral location where human society—royalty, presidency of state, culture, medicine, architecture, the arts, religion and religious magic, and divination—was organized along celestial principles. According to the deported slaves, the *loa* made the voyage from Guinea to the Caribbean and followed their faithful to the colonies. There, without losing their identity, the *loa* were

47

also connected with Catholic saints. In fact, modern Vodou recognizes the Christian God as the supreme deity, and many of the saints intermingle with ancestral *loa*.

The myriad *loa* are divided into two main branches: *rada* and *petro* (these two words refer to both the *loa* in the branches and the rituals that honor them). The Creole word *rada* comes from Arada, the name of a town in Dahomey. *Petro*, on the other hand, is derived from a historical character who lived in Haiti in the middle of the eighteenth century and for some obscure reason took the name of an African tribe whose rites he exalted. Within the *rada* and *petro* branches are categories of *loa* that reflect the various African ethnic groups. They are grouped into families called *nanchon,* or nations.

Spirits from Dahomey who are in principle considered the "good *loa*," also known as *loa* from Guinea, or *loa-Ginen*, are worshiped in *rada*. All Vodou initiation ceremonies appeal to *rada* gods.

Petro honors mainly the spirits of Saint-Domingue itself, who are called the "Creole *loa*." Highly bitter and vengeful, they are more dangerous than the gentle *loa-Ginen*. Creole *loa* are used in the practice of magic. Occasionally, *rada* gods are also invoked in *petro* rituals, but they appear only in their violent aspects. *Petro* gods are ferocious, rough, implacable, and angry. They can cure as well as cast spells and are considered the

THE SPIRITS OF VODOU

supernatural magicians one has to invoke when preparing charms. Any transaction with the Creole *loa* is considered risky and can backfire on the supplicant's intentions: *petro* are pitiless creditors when it comes to collecting the dues owed them for the favors they have granted.

A third and minor set of gods are those grouped in the *kongo* rituals, relating to the *loa* of Bantu (a West African tribe) origin, who are very exuberant deities.

Each *loa* category has its own special drum rhythms, musical instruments, dances, and salutations, and no one can mistake a *rada* ceremony for that of a *petro*. Each *loa* also has one or two days a week that are sacred to him or her, as well as a favorite color.

It is difficult to know the true origin of the gods, their original cosmic role, and how Vodou mythology developed, because the *loa* seem inextricably tied to the everyday affairs of humankind—so much so that the stories of the Vodou gods resemble village gossip, as this or that god intervened in this or that human event. Vodou is more involved with life on earth than it is with the celestial lives of the gods. Inevitably, the main theme of legends and myths revolves around the intervention of the *loa* on behalf of their devotees or the punishment they inflict on those who neglect them.

Among the myriad *loa* that constitute the Vodou pantheon, some assume greater importance than others in all the rituals:

51

THE SPIRITS OF VODOU

PAPA LEGBA (RADA RITUAL)

Papa Legba is the first god to be invoked at the beginning of
every ritual, for he opens the door between the world of the
living and the supernatural world of the gods. At the beginning
of every ceremony, a song is chanted to Papa Legba asking him
to lift the veil between the two worlds:

> Papa Legba ouvri bayé-a pou mwen
> Pou mwen pase
> Lè ma tounen, ma salyié lwa yo.
> [Papa Legba, open the gate for me,
> So I can go through,
> When I return I will pay honor to the *loa*.]

Like Prometheus in Greek mythology, Papa Legba stole God's
secrets and gave them to humans. He protects the entrance of
temples and homes, and can be found at crossroads. In Dahomey
animist religion, Legba acts as the interpreter without whom
humans and gods could not communicate. In Vodou, no gods
would dare to show up at a ritual without having obtained Legba's
permission first. As he holds the key to the supernatural world
he is identified as Saint Peter, as well as with Saint Anthony as
guardian of lost objects. His special days are Fridays and Saturdays.
At noon and midnight Papa Legba turns into a spirit of magic,
and both *rada* and *petro* rituals invoke him. In Cuba he is called

53

Ogu or Elegba; in Brazil he's known as Eshu and is sometimes associated with the Christian devil.

Papa Legba is mostly represented as an old man in rags, pipe in mouth, with a sack thrown over his shoulders. This feeble appearance is deceptive, however—anyone who is possessed by his spirit is thrown to the ground and experiences powerful convulsions.

OGOU THE RED (RADA RITUAL)

Ogou is a *rada* spirit known for his warrior qualities—he is the god of war, labor, and iron. In Cuba he is known as Ogun. Also known as the *loa* of fertility, Ogun has intimate relations with many other *loa*, including Ezili, an Aphrodite-like goddess who personifies beauty and sensuality and lives in the waters. His Christian counterpart is Saint James the Greater, and his special days are Fridays, Saturdays, and Mondays. His favorite color is red, and his element is fire.

BHATALAH (RADA RITUAL)

Also known as Obatalà in Cuba, Bhatalah is the kind father of all the *loa* and of humanity. He rules the mind, is considered the source of wisdom and compassion, and inspires purity of intention. Bhatalah also has a warrior side, through which he enforces justice upon the world. His symbolic color is white, which is often accented with red, purple, and other colors. He is the only *loa* who manifests in both male and female forms.

Baron Samdi and the Gédé Family
(petro ritual)

Baron Samdi is the head of the Gédé family (who are also occasionally honored in the *rada* rituals), a group of spirits who belonged to a clan conquered by the royal family of Dahomey (the original slavers). The spirits followed the clan when it was deported to the plantations in Saint Domingue. The Gédé are the *loa* of death, and dances in their honor take place in both town and country on the first two days of the month of November. The faithful dress up as the Gédé, wearing black clothes and undertakers' outfits, and plugging their nostrils with cotton so that they speak in nasal voices, inspiring both fear and merriment in the faithful. Their favorite dance is the well-known *banda*, characterized by the rotation of the hips and sexy movements. The Gédé are always up to tricks, stealing, lying, and annoying the living. They dress in top hats, bowlers, or straw hats and wear tailcoats as if they were perpetually in grand mourning. The Gédé can be relied on to bring an element of frank gaiety to the most serious rituals, and whenever they appear at a ceremony they are always greeted warmly by the congregation.

AGWÉ AND THE SIMBI (RADA RITUAL)

Agwé is the god of the sea, a kind of Haitian Neptune, who presides over ocean fauna and flora, ships, and fishermen. Sometimes called Agwé-taroyo, he is invoked under the name "Shell of the Sea," "Eel," and "Tadpole of the Pond," and his Christian counterpart is Saint Ulrich. Agwé's emblems are miniature boats, blue or green oars, shells and Madre pores, and small fish. His symbolic color is white, and he is sometimes depicted as a mulatto with green eyes who wears the uniform of a naval officer, white gloves, and a helmet. He loves gunfire, and many thought the salves used to salute the arrival of ships in the harbor of Port-au-Prince were fired in his honor. Thursday is his special day.

Rituals in honor of Agwé are carried out beside the sea, by lakes or rivers. His effigy, usually in the form of a small boat, is then carried in procession. The Whale and the Siren are part of Agwé's "family." A young coquette priestess, very proud of her looks, represents the Siren at rituals. The Whale is said by some to be her mother and, by others, her husband.

Simbi, the guardians of fountains and marshes, are also part of the same family, but are honored in *petro* rituals. The three magi of the Christian nativity also represent them. The *simbi* cannot live without fresh water, and their rituals are always celebrated near springs and fountains. Small children are told

that *simbi* may abduct them and take them underwater to become their servants. When the children grow up, the *simbi* return them to the world of the living and, in reward for their services, bestow upon them the gift of clairvoyance.

DAMBALLAH-WÈDO AND AIDA-WÈDO (RADA RITUAL)

Perhaps the most popular Vodou god is Damballah, the serpent god, who with his wife Aida-wèdo, is most often portrayed in murals in Vodou churches and altars. Damballah is the god of lightning. Being both a terrestrial and aquatic deity, he haunts rivers, springs, and marshes. He is also symbolized by the rainbow, and all offerings to him must be white, his sacred color. His Catholic counterpart is Saint Patrick, who is often depicted ridding Ireland of all its snakes. People possessed by Damballah-wèdo dart out their tongues, crawl on the floor with sinuous, snakelike movements, or climb trees. Damballah does not speak, but whistles. Ogou the Red generally interprets the sacred messages the serpent god transmits to the faithful during possessions. Damballah's special day is Thursday.

His wife Aida-wèdo is the goddess of wealth, luck, and happiness; the Virgin of the Immaculate Conception often symbolizes her. She too loves the color white, and all offerings to her—rice, milk, egg whites—must contain this color. She lives in springs and rivers with her husband and guards the treasure at the end of the rainbow. Her special days are Mondays and Tuesdays.

EZILI (RADA RITUAL)

Ezili is the equivalent of Aphrodite in Vodou. Though originally a sea goddess, in time she became completely divorced from her original attributes and emerged as a personification of feminine grace and beauty. She is coquettish, sensual, pleasure-loving, and extravagant. Every Vodou sanctuary contains a room or a corner dedicated to Ezili; her red and blue dresses as well as her jewelry, toothbrush, comb, lipstick, and perfume are kept there. She loves to seduce and to possess men, and women naturally tend to distrust this beautiful goddess. Ezili's life is a succession of scandals: She has been the "kept woman" of Damballah-wèdo and thus the co-wife of Aida-wèdo. She has also had liaisons with Agwé, Ogou, and many others. Her Christian equivalent is, paradoxically, the Virgin Mary, and her sacred days are Tuesdays and Thursdays.

THE TWINS (PETRO RITUAL)

The Twins, known as *marassa*, hold a special place in the Vodou pantheon beside the *mystères*. Some even claim that they are more powerful than the *loa*. They are always invoked and saluted in every ceremony immediately after Legba. Any family

that includes twins, either living or in its ancestral lines, must serve the *marassa* with special offerings and libations lest they suffer great chastisement. The Vodou twins are extremely demanding and touchy, and they are fussy about the services they demand from the faithful. Their Christian equivalents are Cosmas and Damian, the martyr twins. There is also a link between the *marassa* and rain: the twins can foretell storms and thunderstorms, and if offered enough libations, they can bring rain to a village or region.

Like the *loa*, the *marassa* belong to different *nanchon* (families); there are Guinea, Dahomey, Nago, Ibo, Congo, and Anmine twins. Those born in Haiti are known as Creole *marassa*.

Food and objects offered as libations to the twins must be taken into the woods and placed on the branches of trees rather than on an altar. Possessions by the twins are very rare, but those seized by the *marassa* become childish and capricious, throwing temper tantrums and rolling on the floor.

The Vodou Altar

THE FIRST VODOU TEMPLES were built during the slave era in inaccessible reaches where slave owners would never go. In some respects this need for secrecy has survived since those years of fear, and today many Vodou temples remain hidden in basements or in secret locations. In Haiti, temples to the loa are scattered everywhere, especially in the countryside.

The Vodou temple, called the *oufó*, is more of a ceremonial hut than a church. Sometimes the *oufó* resembles a small village with several buildings; other times it is as small as a covered area that shelters the *loa* and houses the family of the priest. What makes the *oufó* recognizable from the outside is the peristyle, a shed or covered area where Vodou dances and ceremonies are conducted no matter what the season or weather. The roof of the peristyle is held by brightly painted posts. The one in the center is called the *poteau mitan* (the center post). Most ritual dances pivot around it. Its ceremonial role is as a doorway to the spirit world, a sort of ladder that the *loa* descend to communicate with the faithful on earth. The post is usually embedded in a conical or cylindrical cement base, on which ceremonial items are set during services. Ritual drums are also usually hung on the walls of the peristyle. Traditional *oufós* sometimes have one recess for the *rada loa* and another for the *petro loa*.

The "chamber of the gods," the inner sanctum of the *oufó* that houses the patron spirits, opens to one side of the peristyle. The outer façade of the *oufó*, which forms the back of the peristyle, is decorated with paintings and brightly colored murals depicting the symbols of the *loa* and ornamental motifs. Frequently, portraits of the president of Haiti and other important ministers are also hung there to enhance this place of power. The inner sanctum, called *caye-mystères* (also known as *bagi* or *sobadji*), is a room backed by one or more stone altars. The altars are sometimes arranged in tiers to house more *loa*. Basins and sinks used for honoring aquatic spirits are placed on tables. At first sight, the inner sanctum resembles a junk shop: jars, pots, and dishes with food are placed on the different tiers of the altar as offerings for various *loa*. The spirits receive gifts of all sorts: wine, liquor, water, playing cards, pieces of colored cloth, rattles, candles, shells, photographs of family members or friends in need of cures or blessings, color prints that evoke specific events, charms, bags containing special treasures, jewels, and anything and everything that takes the fancy of the *hungan*. There are no specific rules as to how to adorn an altar. It is up to the individual's imagination as to what objects and decorations are deemed most suitable for each *loa* honored. An altar to Ezili, for instance, can be dressed

as a boudoir, and an altar for Baron Samdi can be housed inside a coffin.

On the altar are effigies of the *loa*, often represented by clay statues dressed up with dolls' clothes or adorned with expensive cuts of fabrics. Sometimes statues of Catholic saints become the images of Vodou *loa*; a mixture of Christian objects, such as rosaries and crosses, and Vodou decorations adorn them.

Cocks, hens, pigeons, small goats, and guinea fowl traditionally live outside Haitian *oufós*, waiting for the day of sacrifice; there is often a slim difference between a Vodou sanctuary and a farm.

The Vodou Ritual

THE RELATIONSHIP between the loa and humankind is easy and constant. Gods and goddesses communicate with the faithful either by possessing an individual who then becomes the *loa*'s mouthpiece or by appearing in dreams or in mysterious encounters where they take human form to perform a deed or deliver a message. Also, priests and priestesses have the power to call the *loa* down into jars and bottles decorated brightly with beads and paints to make them all the more attractive for mystical embottlement. From these spirit bottles, the gods can converse with those who wish to question them.

All rituals and consecrations occur in the *oufó*, in which the *hungan* exercises absolute power. Vodou priests and priestesses interpret the language of the *loa*, serve as psychological counselors for the members of the congregation, and also practice herbal medicine. Their power is believed to have been passed down from their predecessors by means of dreams or by illnesses that indicate their vocation. Each *hungan* has been initiated into his or her office by a special ceremony that takes place after nine days of complete confinement, the culmination of a long period of training under another priest or priestess in the *oufó*. All *hungans*

cultivate relations with one another and sometimes work together
on particularly difficult cases of illness or curses. Hungans
mainly deal with the good *loa* and never practice black magic,
although there exist priests and priestesses who "practice with
both hands," meaning they are also sorcerers. It is believed that
the *loa* will turn against *hungans* who are charlatans or who abuse
their power and harm the faithful. Hungans treat only the illnesses
that are believed to have supernatural causes, such as broken hearts,
nightmares, misfortunes, lost lovers, troubled marriages, and
business setbacks. These and a myriad of other human afflictions
are controlled by the *loa* and can be cured in the *oufó*, which
often resembles a kind of clinic for human misfortune.

The *hungan* is assisted by several members of his "society,"
the helpers in his or her *oufó*. A ring of worshipers dressed in
pure white (called *ounsi*, or "initiates") forms around the *poteau-
mitan*. In charge of ritual singing and dancing, they galvanize the
atmosphere of ceremonies under the direction of the *ongenikón*,
or "queen singer." The master of ceremonies is called the *laplas*;
the guardian of the sacrificial animals is known as the *bête-charge*.
There is also an administrator of the *oufó* whose job it is to collect
the money paid for any ceremony, healing, or interpretation of
divine messages. Also present is a *pitit-fèy*, or diligent servant,
who helps with the setup of ceremonies and rituals.

Vodou ceremonies, called services, take place at marked

annual holidays and on the special days of the *loa* being appealed
to for cures or wishes. The Vodou liturgical calendar closely
follows that of the Catholic Church: for example, the *bains de
chance* (lucky baths) fall on Christmas; the Epiphany on January
6 is Vodou's New Year's Day; All Saints on November 1 is the
festival of the Gédé, the spirits of death; and the day dedicated
to Our Lady of Mount Carmel (the Virgin Mary) on July 16 is
Ezili's day.

THE VODOU SERVICE

A typical vodou ceremony has two main parts. First come the
rites of entry, in which Papa Legba is asked to open the door
between the world of the spirits and that of humankind. The
sacred objects in the *oufó* are greeted, including the ceremonial
drums, which, together with the dancing and singing that begin
immediately, play a crucial role in the service, creating rhythms
that bring the heartbeats of the faithful and of the *loa* together.
The sacred objects are oriented to the four cardinal points in
order to define the sacred space in which the ceremony is
taking place. Finally, the different *loa* that are being invited to
the service are invoked with long litanies and Catholic prayers.
The air in the peristyle is usually warmed by this first part of
the ceremony, as everyone is drumming, singing, and dancing
around the *poteau-mitan*.

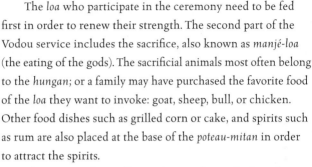

The *loa* who participate in the ceremony need to be fed first in order to renew their strength. The second part of the Vodou service includes the sacrifice, also known as *manjé-loa* (the eating of the gods). The sacrificial animals most often belong to the *hungan*; or a family may have purchased the favorite food of the *loa* they want to invoke: goat, sheep, bull, or chicken. Other food dishes such as grilled corn or cake, and spirits such as rum are also placed at the base of the *poteau-mitan* in order to attract the spirits.

The person who is offering the sacrifice to the *loa* is known as the *commanditaire*. The *commanditaire*, whose head is always wrapped in a red handkerchief, offers the specially prepared dishes to the sacrificial animals; if the animals eat the food, it means that the loa have accepted the sacrifice.

The sacrificial animal is then ritually prepared for the sacrifice. A member of the *oufó*, who has taken purifying baths before the ceremony, washes the animal's head, neck, and feet with an infusion made with leaves, and then perfumes it. After killing the animal, he or she drinks a few drops of blood and draws a cross with it on his or her forehead. The animal is then directed to the four points of the compass, presenting the sacrifice to the supernatural powers of the four "sides." It is finally carved and cooked outside the peristyle in the courtyard of the *oufó*.

At this point in the service, the most crucial events take place. The *hungan* draws the *vévé*, a beautiful symbolic drawing in white chalk, on the ground after arriving at its design during the course of the ceremony. Then, with the beating of the drums and special songs, the *loa* arrive. The faithful who have been entered by the *loa* are seized by a fit of possession.

Possession is perhaps the fundamental phenomenon of Vodou. Through possession, the divine and the human intersect. A *loa* moves into the head of an individual, having first dislodged the "good big angel" (*gros bon ange*), one of the two souls believed to inhabit every human being. The trembling and convulsions that are characteristic of the opening stages of the trance are a clear sign that the soul of the individual is being dispossessed by a *loa*. As the head and the limbs convulse, the individual becomes the instrument of the god or goddess, and their relationship can be compared to that of rider and horse. In fact, it is said that a *loa* is "mounting" or "saddling" his *chual* (horse) during possession. It seems as if the spirit is dancing inside the body of the devotee. The intensity of the beginning stages of the trance varies according to the character of the spirit who is possessing the human and the spiritual maturity of the person being possessed. The *petro loa*, for instance, rush into bodies with the speed and violence of a hurricane. The *hungan* and the crowd of the faithful catch the possessed if they fall and succor them if the convulsions become violent. Possession can be short or long; there is no way of telling whether the god or goddess will be incarnate a few minutes, hours, or days. Sometimes onlookers to the Vodou service also fall into trances.

The officiating *hungan* offers the *loa* more food and interprets their confused language for the *commanditaire*, asking questions and drawing answers from the spirits. Perfectly schooled in the habits of the *loa*, the *hungan* communicates with them through gestures the spirits can understand and respond to.

The appearance of the gods at the service is the hallmark of a successful Vodou ritual. Without their presence, the faithful are left without protection and guidance, and they can fall into misfortune without their divine counsel. The *loa* exist to protect the living from danger, be it spiritual or material, and can be appealed to in simple rituals and offerings.

Make Your Own Vodou Altar

VODOU is, above all, the religion of the personal, of the intimate, of the direct relationship between you and the spirits. Although traditional Vodou always employs a *hungan* to call the *loa* into the *oufú* and to interpret their messages, Vodou can also be the channel for an individual connection with your favorite god or goddess.

This chapter gives suggestions on rituals and formulas that honor the *rada loa*, dealing exclusively with good magic that extends positive energy to everyone and everything. The chapter also excludes animal sacrifice, as this is nowadays practiced only in the countryside in Haiti; most priests and priestesses no longer include it in their rites. The rituals and offerings suggested here are drawn from the modern practice of Vodou for everyone to use without causing harm or danger to themselves or others. It is positive, joyful Vodou.

BUILDING YOUR ALTAR

Creating your own Vodou altar is not difficult, as there are no set rules for what *loa* should be included or how the altar should be decorated.

Vodou altars often resemble small theaters placed on a table in the corner of a bedroom. They have a backing, which can be made of a beautiful textile or piece of cardboard painted in bright colors, and are open at the front. The floor of the altar can also be decorated, perhaps with *vévés* drawn symbolically in white chalk to establish the sacred ground.

The altar can be decorated with special objects that are magical to you, such as shells, stones, bells, small images, a container with water to attract aquatic spirits, leaves or a piece of tree bark, a magical instrument made of bone, sacred feathers, rattles, or small drums. Anything that invites or suggests to you the intersection of the spirit and the human world can be part of the altar.

Vodou altars are often crowded with objects honoring several *loa*, who are represented by statues of their Catholic saint counterparts. For instance, Ezili appears on most altars as a statuette of the Virgin Mary, and Papa Legba as Saint Peter. Statues of Catholic saints can be found either in specialized shops or through the Internet. It is also good to make your own Vodou statuettes out of clay, modeling with your own hands and imagination, since they are imbued with the attention, time, and intent you have dedicated to their creation.

Altars must have decorated bottles, such as the one that comes with this book, for the mystical embottlement of the *loa*.

Traditionally, bottles are decorated with many tiny beads, arranged in patterns or simply at random to make the bottle more attractive, but they can also be painted. A basket of fresh flowers as well as some incense sticks are a nice addition to any altar, as well as candles that will remain lit during your Vodou rituals.

A Voudou "wish box" is a smaller, portable altar. This can be constructed from a cardboard box, perhaps covered in cloth or silk, that is then decorated with the symbols and colors of your favorite *loa*. You may keep fetishes or ritual keepsakes empowered with your magic wish in the box to attract the *loa* to make it come true.

There are also a number of Vodou ritual objects that you can make up on your own or purchase to help you in your magic rituals:

GRIS-GRIS BAGS

Gris-gris bags are little bags made from a square piece of silk, satin, or velvet cloth. They contain sacred herbs, a talisman, perhaps a semiprecious stone or a crystal, and some drops of essential oil. Place the contents in the bags and then tie them shut with a ribbon as you make your magic wish or blessing. *Gris-gris* bags can be made and blessed for every kind of wish: love affairs; new births; protection; a new home; peace of mind; success with a new enterprise, meeting, or exam; good health. They bring good luck and can be carried with you wherever you go.

RITUAL DOLLS

Small ritual dolls are cloth dolls made of brightly colored material—red, green, blue, white, or black. To make a ritual doll, cut out two identical doll-shaped pieces of cloth, stuff them with wool or cotton wool, and stitch them together. These are to be used only for good and positive magic. Pins are inserted in to drive out illness, misfortune, suffering, and the effects of negative energy. Invite positive energy to replace what you have banished and to restore harmony and well-being.

HOUSEHOLD SPIRITS

The *loa* can be called into an object to provide protection at home. Household spirit figures work especially well in children's rooms; you can encourage the younger generation to help you in crafting them. Using papier-mâché, make up the masks of your favorite spirits and adorn them with feathers, jewelry, paint, shells, and other materials you like. Then hang the masks by the window in the room you wish to protect.

PAPA LEGBA HEADS

Papa Legba is the *loa* protecting all crossroads, whether they be life choices, points of destiny, everyday circumstances, the boundaries between the sacred and the profane, or the corners and entrances to your home or sacred space. A Papa Legba head

is traditionally made of a round stone with one side that is flat enough to be able to stand on a surface. The head is decorated with cowry shells for the eyes and a painted mouth. Clay can also be used to make one of these ritual heads. You can fashion it as a candle-holder for your altar.

JUJUS

Jujus are objects blessed to keep evil and negativity away. They can be anything: talismans, statuettes of the *loa*, sacred stones, precious objects, fetishes, or any other thing that can hold your blessing and positive, protective magic. Jujus are wonderful protective objects that you can keep on your desk at the office or on your bedside table, or that you can present someone as a gift. Children too love jujus for their own important moments at school or for good luck on an exam.

THE RITUAL KIT

You should have a Vodou ritual kit always ready in advance. This will include a candle that has never been lit before, a *gris-gris* bag never used before, some incense sticks, and a ritual doll. Keep your ritual kit in a special, sacred place. You may want to make up a Vodou box where you keep your magical objects, or they can be wrapped in a beautiful cloth and kept on your altar.

vODoU

VODOU GIFT BASKET

Make a Vodou gift basket to give to friends or loved ones. Place the ritual objects that you decide to include in a basket or small straw hamper. The objects could be any of the above, plus incense sticks, a candle, and perhaps a blessing written in your own handwriting.

PREPARING FOR THE RITUALS

While you prepare for your Vodou ritual—lighting the candles and incense sticks, placing fresh flowers on the altar, making the food you will serve on special platters to the *loa*—it is important that you prepare your intent also. In order to relax and quiet your mind, you may want to listen to some African songs and chants whose wonderful resonant quality will help you enter the spirit of positive Vodou. This spiritual preparation, opening your mind and heart to Vodou, is essential for the success of your ritual.

Appeal to Papa Legba and ask him to lift the veil between the visible and invisible world of the spirits. You can use his traditional formula found on page 53 or make up your own sacred words.

Make your intent clear. Visualize what you would like to happen, keep your mind focused on the result, and allow the image to become more clearly defined with each heartbeat. You may want to play some drums at this time, as their rhythm will

86

synchronize both your breath and your heartbeat to the spirits of Vodou.

Once your intent has become completely clear in your mind's eye, wish positively for its attainment and ask the *loa* for their assistance in granting this wish. Surround yourself and your vision with a pure golden light and make your wish in the heart, the most positive chamber of your being.

Now offer food to the *loa* by placing it on the altar, and say a prayer or blessing to conclude your ritual. You can make up your own formulas to personalize the ritual, finding your own way to create a dialogue and to be intimate with the powerful *loa* of Africa.

To end your ritual, sit silently, breathing steadily, attuning your nervous system to the magic wish you have just expressed. In every gesture, in every action, know that there is grace and gratitude.

May Vodou and the *loa* bring you infinite blessings and well-being!

SPIRIT BOTTLE RITUAL

The bright colors of the spirit bottle you find in this box will attract the *loa* to it, and they will empower this sacred object. Place it somewhere prominent, preferably in a clear space so that its power is not diminished. You can also place it on your altar, but give it prominence in some way.

Spirit bottles are used traditionally to converse with the *loa*. Some preparation is needed before you are ready to speak with a deity. Sit peacefully and hold the bottle in your hands. Allow your mind and breathing to slow down and attune to the ritual you are about to make.

Allow your question to arise from your heart; it needs to be simple and clear. You can ask one question at a time, wait for the answer, then ask the next question. Don't attempt too much in one session.

Whisper your question, and imagine that you are putting it out for examination by the *loa*. You are sending it out to the universe. Wait for the answer, which will form slowly within you. You will know the answer rather than hear it. Wait a few minutes before asking your next question.

The answers given by the *loa* may require you to meditate upon them for a few days. If you have asked about a course of action to be taken, for instance, don't act immediately, but rather wait for a few days, grow into the new attitude required by the situation, and then act. If you have asked about how to behave with another person, again, wait for a few days, meditate on the appropriate steps to be taken, and then move into the new situation. You are following a sacred path that cannot be rushed, but must be followed with consideration and meditation. The *loa* will only give answers that are entirely right for you, your

needs, your personality, the responsibilities you carry at the moment, and the spiritual tasks you can achieve. Trust in their answers and they will offer the right path to follow.

Further Reading

Brown, Karen McCarthy. *Mama Lola: Vodou Priestess in Brooklyn.* Los Angeles: University of California Press, 1991.

Cosentino, Donald J., ed. *Sacred Arts of Haitian Vodou.* Los Angeles: University of California Los Angeles, Fowler Museum of Cultural History, 1995.

Davis, Wade. *The Serpent and the Rainbow.* London: Collins, 1986.

Deren, Maya. *The Voodoo Gods.* Saint Albans, U.K.: Paladin Press, 1975.

Gilfond, Henry. *Voodoo: Its Origins and Practices.* New York and London: Franklin Watts, 1976.

Hurbon, Laennec. *Vodou: Truth and Fantasy.* London: Thames and Hudson, 1995.

Kerboull, Jean. *Voodoo and Magic Practices.* Translated from the French by John Shaw. London: Barne & Jenkins, 1978.

Laguerre, Michael. *Voodoo and Politics in Haiti.* London: Macmillan, 1989.

———. *Voodoo Heritage.* London: Sage Publications, 1980.

Métraux, Alfred. *Vodou in Haiti.* New York: Schocken Books, 1972.

Rigaud, Milo. *Secrets of Vodou.* San Francisco: City Lights, 1969.

Williams, Sheldon. *Voodoo and the Art of Haiti.* London: Morland Lee, 1969.

Art Acknowledgments

Thanks go to the following people for their help with the Haitian art in this book: Ned Hopkins, Tony Fisher at Indigo Arts, Legrand Montfleury at HaitianPainting.com, and Bill Bollendorf at Galerie Macondo.

Box lid, platform, and page 87: Tools of Vodou, by Roger Francois; courtesy of Galerie Macondo, Pittsburgh

Front endpapers: Ceremonie, by Jean-Louis Maxan; courtesy of Indigo Arts, Philadelphia

Page 6: Ceremonie Vodou, by Theard Aladin; courtesy of Indigo Arts, Philadelphia

Page 8: The Houngan, by Theard Aladin; courtesy of Galerie Macondo, Pittsburgh

Page 14: Historical Scene, by Alexandre Gregoire; courtesy of Indigo Arts, Philadelphia

Page 17: The King of Dahomey's Levee, by Francis Chesham, 1793; © The British Library/Heritage Images, London

Page 18: Vodou in Benin, by Michel Renaudeau; courtesy of Hoa-qui, Paris

Page 21: Vodou in Benin, by Maurice Ascani; courtesy of
Hoa-qui, Paris

Pages 24–25: Vodou in Benin, by Maurice Ascani; courtesy of
Hoa-qui, Paris

Page 26: Vodou in Benin, by Maurice Ascani; courtesy of
Hoa-qui, Paris

Page 29: Vodou ceremony in Haiti, by Chantal Regnault;
courtesy of Explorer, Paris

Page 30: Vodou ceremony at Sylva Joseph Peristyle, Port au
Prince, Haiti; by Maggie Steber, Miami

Page 32: Ceremony feuille (leaf ceremony), Hounsis perform
healing dance, Haiti; by Maggie Steber, Miami

Page 34: Ceremony by the Sea, by Theard Aladin; courtesy of
Galerie Macondo, Pittsburgh

Page 36–37: Dancing, by Kesnel Franklin, 1970; courtesy of
HaitianPainting.com, Summit, WA

Page 41: Why Us?, by Marc-Antoine Gaston, 1986; courtesy of
HaitianPainting.com, Summit, WA

Page 42: Aida Wedo and Medji, by Frantz Zephirin; courtesy of
Galerie Macondo, Pittsburgh

Page 44: In a Vodou temple, Haiti; by Maggie Steber, Miami

Page 46: Loas, by Louisiane Saint-Fleurant; courtesy of Ned
Hopkins, London

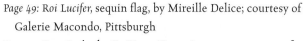

Page 49: Roi Lucifer, sequin flag, by Mireille Delice; courtesy of Galerie Macondo, Pittsburgh

Page 50: Papa Legba, by St. Pierre Toussaint, 1970; courtesy of HaitianPainting.com, Summit, WA

Page 52: Papa Zaca, by Gerard Valcin; courtesy of Ned Hopkins, London

Page 57: Baron Samedi, by Theard Aladin; courtesy of Galerie Macondo, Pittsburgh

Page 58: Ezili Freda, by Jonas Profil; courtesy of Galerie Macondo, Pittsburgh

Page 61: Damhala Wouedo, by André Pierre; courtesy of Ned Hopkins, London

Page 62: Marassa with Erzuli Dantor, by Francoise Eliassaint; courtesy of Galerie Macondo, Pittsburgh

Page 64: Vodou altar, Haiti; by Maggie Steber, Miami

Page 67: Vodou altar of André Pierre, Haiti; by Maggie Steber, Miami

Page 68: Day of the Dead, Guede ceremony, Haiti; by Maggie Steber, Miami

Page 70: Mambo, by André Pierre, 2000; courtesy of HaitianPainting.com, Summit, WA

Page 72: Vodou in Haiti, by Chantal Regnault; courtesy of Explorer, Paris

Page 75: Vodou altar, by Martha Cooper

ART ACKNOWLEDGEMENTS

Page 77: Vodou in Haiti, by Chantal Regnault; courtesy of Explorer, Paris

Page 80: Vodou altar in Haiti, by Chantal Regnault; courtesy of Explorer, Paris

Page 90: Vodou altar, by Martha Cooper

Page 92: Dancing Loa, by Gerard Paul; courtesy of Ned Hopkins, London

Back Endpapers: Marriage du La Sirene et Agoué, by Madsen Mompremier; courtesy of Ned Hopkins, London